From

Classroom

to Podium

A Student's Guide to
Powerful Public Speaking
& Presentation Skills

Speak, Influence, Succeed!

Gerard Assey

From Classroom to Podium:
A Student's Guide to Powerful Public
Speaking & Presentation Skills
By
Gerard Assey
© Copyright 2023 by Author

Published by:
Gerard Assey
19/18, Palli Arasan Street
Anna Nagar East
Chennai - 600 102

(Image courtesy: storyset on Freepik: 'https://www.freepik.com'
Thank You)

Table of Contents

Preface

Welcome to the world of effective presentations and confident public speaking! This book: **'From Classroom to Podium:** *A Student's Guide to Powerful Public Speaking & Presentation Skills'* is your comprehensive guide to mastering the art of public speaking and presentation skills, tailored specifically for students like you.

In today's rapidly evolving world, the ability to communicate ideas, inspire others, and confidently express yourself is a skill that opens doors to countless opportunities. Whether you're a student navigating the academic landscape, preparing for job interviews, or aspiring to be a future leader, this book is designed to equip you with the tools, techniques, and strategies you need to excel in the art of public speaking.

In the pages that follow, you will embark on a transformative journey that covers every aspect of public speaking and presentations. From conquering the fear of public speaking to crafting compelling speeches, and from mastering body language to using visual aids effectively, each chapter is carefully designed to empower you with practical knowledge and actionable steps.

Our aim is not only to provide you with a wealth of information but also to engage you with captivating examples, insightful quotes, and interactive exercises. These exercises are not just theoretical; they are your opportunities to apply what you learn, practice your skills, and ultimately become a confident and persuasive speaker.

Throughout this book, we draw inspiration from accomplished speakers, successful leaders, and individuals who have faced and conquered their own speaking challenges. You will find their stories, insights, and journeys woven into the fabric of this book, offering you valuable perspectives and real-world lessons.

Public speaking and presentation skills are not reserved for a select few; they are attainable by anyone willing to invest time and effort into their development. As you progress through these pages, remember that becoming an effective speaker is not an endpoint but a lifelong journey. Your growth as a communicator will continue long after you've turned the last page.

We invite you to embrace this journey with enthusiasm and an open mind. Challenge yourself, step out of your comfort zone, and see the transformation that awaits you. Public speaking is not just a skill; it's a catalyst for personal and professional growth.

We hope this book serves as a trusted companion on your path to becoming a confident speaker and communicator. May it empower you to stand before any audience, convey your message with conviction, and make a lasting impact.

Best wishes on your journey to confident and influential public speaking!

Importance of this Skill
Benefits & Repercussions

Public speaking and presentation skills are crucial for students, and honing these skills offers a wide range of benefits, while neglecting them can have significant repercussions. Here's an overview of why it's essential for students to focus on developing these skills:

Benefits:

Effective Communication: Public speaking skills enable students to convey their ideas, thoughts, and messages clearly and persuasively. This ability is invaluable in both academic and professional settings.

Confidence Building: As students gain competence in public speaking, their self-confidence naturally grows. This newfound confidence extends beyond the stage and positively impacts various aspects of their lives.

Career Advancement: The ability to present ideas and influence others is a valuable asset in the job market. Strong presentation skills can lead to better job opportunities and career advancement.

Leadership Development: Effective public speakers often become leaders. They inspire and motivate others, whether in the classroom, workplace, or community.

Enhanced Academic Performance: Improved communication skills can boost academic performance. Students who can present their ideas effectively tend to excel in assignments, discussions, and class presentations.

Critical Thinking: Crafting a compelling presentation requires critical thinking and problem-solving skills. Students learn to structure their thoughts logically and support their arguments with evidence.

Influence and Persuasion: Public speaking skills empower students to persuade others and advocate for their viewpoints. This is vital in debates, negotiations, and discussions.

Networking: Effective speakers are more likely to engage in networking opportunities. They can connect with peers, professors, and professionals, expanding their social and professional circles.

Emotional Intelligence: Public speaking often involves connecting with an audience on an emotional level. Students learn to read and respond to the emotions and needs of their listeners.

Global Perspective: In an interconnected world, the ability to communicate with diverse audiences is crucial. Public speaking skills allow students to engage with people from various backgrounds and cultures.

Repercussions of Neglecting Public Speaking and Presentation Skills:

Missed Opportunities: Without strong presentation skills, students may miss out on opportunities to excel academically and professionally.

Reduced Confidence: Avoiding public speaking can erode self-confidence and increase anxiety when faced with speaking engagements.

Limited Career Growth: In the professional world, poor communication can hinder career growth and limit access to leadership roles.

Ineffective Advocacy: Students may struggle to advocate for their ideas, limiting their ability to influence decisions or create change.

Difficulty in Interviews: Job interviews often require effective communication. Students lacking presentation skills may struggle to make a positive impression.

Academic Challenges: In an academic setting, the inability to present findings or arguments coherently can result in lower grades and missed opportunities for research or scholarship.

Weakened Social Interactions: Effective communication is vital in personal relationships. Students may find it challenging to express themselves or connect with others if they lack public speaking skills.

As seen above, focusing on public speaking and presentation skills is essential for students because it not only enhances their academic and professional prospects but also contributes to personal growth and confidence. Neglecting these skills can limit opportunities, hinder career advancement, and impede effective communication in various aspects of life.

Assessment before Reading and Practicing

Assess Yourself: Self-Evaluation of Presentation Skills

Content Clarity (Scale: 1-5)
- ✓ Rate how clearly you believe you can communicate your ideas and messages.
- ✓ 1 = Unclear and confusing, 5 = Extremely clear and concise.

Confidence Level (Scale: 1-5)
- ✓ Assess your confidence when speaking in front of an audience.
- ✓ 1 = Very nervous and unsure, 5 = Extremely confident and poised.

Audience Engagement (Scale: 1-5)
- ✓ Rate your ability to engage your audience and maintain their interest.
- ✓ 1 = Ineffective at engaging, 5 = Highly effective at engaging.

Use of Visual Aids (Scale: 1-5)
- ✓ Evaluate your proficiency in using visual aids like slides or props.
- ✓ 1 = Poor use of visuals, 5 = Excellent use of visuals.

Body Language and Nonverbal Communication (Scale: 1-5)
- ✓ Assess your body language, gestures, and eye contact during presentations.
- ✓ 1 = Poor nonverbal communication, 5 = Excellent nonverbal communication.

Vocal Delivery (Scale: 1-5)
- ✓ Rate your vocal skills, including pitch, pace, and modulation.

✓ 1 = Ineffective vocal delivery, 5 = Outstanding vocal delivery.

Time Management (Scale: 1-5)
- ✓ Evaluate your ability to stay within time limits during presentations.
- ✓ 1 = Consistently exceed time limits, 5 = Always stay within time limits.

Handling Q&A Sessions (Scale: 1-5)
- ✓ Assess your performance during Q&A sessions, including your ability to answer questions confidently.
- ✓ 1 = Struggle with Q&A, 5 = Excellently handle Q&A.

Overall Presentation Skills (Scale: 1-10)
- ✓ Provide an overall rating of your presentation skills before reading and practicing.
- ✓ 1 = Extremely poor, 10 = Exceptional.

Peer or Instructor Evaluation (Optional)
You can also ask a peer or instructor to evaluate your presentation skills based on the criteria above.

The World of Public Speaking

Why Public Speaking Matters

Public speaking is an indispensable skill that holds immense importance in both personal and professional spheres. It's the art of conveying ideas, stories, and information to an audience effectively. Here's why mastering this skill is crucial:

Engaging Example: Imagine you are in a job interview, and the interviewer asks you to present your qualifications and experiences. Your ability to communicate confidently and persuasively could be the deciding factor in landing your dream job.

Quote: *"The spoken word is perhaps the most powerful tool humankind has ever created. It can be used to inspire, to inform, and to persuade. It is a skill that can shape destinies."* – Brian Tracy

Action Plan: Developing Awareness

- ✓ Reflect on your personal experiences with public speaking. What positive or negative memories do you have?
- ✓ List three situations in which you believe public speaking skills would be valuable.
- ✓ Set a clear goal for what you want to achieve with improved public speaking skills.

Overcoming the Fear of Public Speaking

The fear of public speaking, known as glossophobia, affects many individuals. However, it can be conquered with the right approach. Here's how to face this fear head-on:

Engaging Example: Imagine you have to give a presentation in front of your class, and your heart races, palms sweat, and you can hardly speak. This fear is common, but it's something you can overcome.

Quote: *"The only thing we have to fear is fear itself."* – Franklin D. Roosevelt

Action Plan: Conquering Fear
- ✓ Identify the specific aspects of public speaking that make you anxious (e.g., standing in front of a crowd, fear of forgetting your speech).
- ✓ Gradually expose yourself to these situations in a safe environment. Start by speaking in front of a mirror or recording yourself.
- ✓ Practice deep breathing and relaxation techniques before speaking engagements.

The Power of Effective Communication

Effective communication is at the core of public speaking. It's not just about talking; it's about conveying your message in a way that resonates with your audience. Here's why it matters:

Engaging Example: Consider two friends giving you advice on buying a new smartphone. One friend rambles on with technical jargon, while the other explains the benefits in simple terms, helping you make an informed decision. The latter friend's effective communication had a significant impact.

Quote: *"The most important thing in communication is hearing what isn't said."* – Peter Drucker

Action Plan: Enhancing Communication
- ✓ Understand the importance of active listening. Practice listening to others without interrupting.
- ✓ Experiment with different communication styles (e.g., assertive, empathetic) and assess how they affect your interactions.

✓ Start a journal to record your thoughts and observations on communication in everyday life.

By delving into the world of public speaking, students will not only conquer their fears but also unlock the potential to become influential and persuasive communicators. This chapter sets the stage for the journey ahead, emphasizing the significance of public speaking, addressing common fears, and laying the foundation for effective communication.

Understanding Your Audience

This chapter equips students with practical strategies to connect with their audience, ensuring their message is not only heard but also understood and valued.

Identifying Your Audience

Understanding your audience is the cornerstone of effective communication. Whether you're giving a speech, presentation, or even having a one-on-one conversation, knowing your audience is crucial. Here's why:

Engaging Example: Imagine you are asked to give a speech about climate change to two different audiences: a group of scientists and a group of elementary school students. Your approach, language, and content should vary significantly to cater to the unique needs and interests of each audience.

Quote: *"The success of your presentation will be judged not by the knowledge you send, but by what the listener receives."* – Lilly Walters

Action Plan: Audience Analysis

✓ Before your next presentation or conversation, take a few minutes to research your audience. What are their demographics (age, gender, background)?

✓ What are their interests and concerns related to the topic?

✓ Create an audience profile sheet that outlines key information about your audience, such as their needs, expectations, and potential objections.

Tailoring Your Message to Your Audience
Once you've identified your audience, the next step is to tailor your message to resonate with them. Here's how:
Engaging Example: Think of a time when you heard a speaker who seemed completely disconnected from the audience. Perhaps they used complex jargon that nobody understood. Tailoring your message prevents this and keeps your audience engaged.
Quote: *"The two words 'information' and 'communication' are often used interchangeably, but they signify quite different things. Information is giving out; communication is getting through."* – Sydney J. Harris

Action Plan: Customizing Your Message
- ✓ After identifying your audience, brainstorm ways to make your message relevant to them. What examples, anecdotes, or statistics can you use to connect with their interests or concerns?
- ✓ Avoid using technical jargon or overly complex language if your audience is not familiar with it. Aim for clarity and simplicity in your message.
- ✓ Test your message with a friend or colleague who represents your audience to gather feedback on its effectiveness.

Building Empathy and Connection
Empathy is the ability to understand and share the feelings of another. Building a connection with your audience through empathy can make your message more impactful.

Engaging Example: Consider a motivational speaker who shares a personal story of overcoming adversity. By expressing vulnerability and showing empathy for the struggles of the audience, a deep emotional connection is formed.

Quote: *"To empathize with someone is to see their pain, to feel it with them, to help carry it."* – Daniel H. Pink

Action Plan: Developing Empathy
- ✓ Practice active listening in your everyday conversations. Pay attention not only to the words but also to the emotions and body language of the speaker.
- ✓ Before your next presentation, spend time reflecting on the emotions and concerns your audience might have. How can you address these in your message?
- ✓ Share personal stories or anecdotes that resonate with the experiences of your audience. Vulnerability can create a powerful connection.

Understanding your audience, tailoring your message to their needs, and building empathy are essential skills for any communicator.

Topic Selection and Research

This part will equip students with the skills to choose compelling topics, conduct thorough research, and maintain academic integrity through proper citation practices.

Choosing a Relevant and Engaging Topic

Selecting the right topic is the foundation of a successful presentation. Your topic should be both relevant to your audience and interesting to you as the speaker. Here's why this step is crucial:

Engaging Example: Imagine you have to give a presentation on renewable energy to a group of environmental enthusiasts. A topic like "The Future of Solar Power" would likely capture their interest more than a generic topic like "Energy Sources."

Quote: *"Choose a subject you are passionate about because, when you love what you do, you will never work a day in your life."* – Confucius

Action Plan: Topic Selection

- ✓ Brainstorm a list of potential topics that interest you or relate to your audience's interests.
- ✓ Narrow down your list by considering the relevance, significance, and potential impact of each topic.
- ✓ Choose a topic that aligns with your passions and your audience's needs.

Conducting Thorough Research

Once you've chosen your topic, thorough research is essential to provide accurate and credible information. Here's why research matters:

Engaging Example: Suppose you're delivering a speech about a historical event, like the moon landing. Accurate research ensures that your audience gains a deep understanding of the topic, leading to a more engaging and informative presentation.

Quote: *"Research is formalized curiosity. It is poking and prying with a purpose."* – Zora Neale Hurston

Action Plan: Research Techniques
- ✓ Start by gathering information from reputable sources such as books, academic journals, and trusted websites.
- ✓ Organize your research into key points or arguments that support your topic.
- ✓ Verify the credibility of your sources and cross-reference information to ensure accuracy.

Citing Sources and Avoiding Plagiarism
Giving credit to the sources you use in your presentation is essential to maintain credibility and avoid plagiarism. Here's why proper citation is important:

Engaging Example: Imagine you found an insightful quote from a renowned scientist that perfectly illustrates your point. Citing the source not only gives credit to the original thinker but also adds authority to your presentation.

Quote: *"To steal ideas from one person is plagiarism; to steal from many is research."* – Wilson Mizner

Action Plan: Proper Citation and Avoiding Plagiarism
- ✓ Familiarize yourself with the citation style required by your institution or organization

✓ Keep a detailed record of all sources you use, including author names, publication dates, and page numbers.
✓ Create a works cited or references page and follow the citation guidelines meticulously.

By following these steps, students can ensure their presentations are both engaging and credible, leaving a lasting impact on their audience.

Structuring Your Presentation

We now get into structuring presentations effectively, from grabbing audience's attention with a compelling introduction to leaving a lasting impression with a memorable conclusion.

Crafting a Strong Introduction

Your presentation's introduction is your opportunity to capture your audience's attention, set the tone, and establish your credibility as a speaker. Here's why crafting a strong introduction is vital:

Engaging Example: Imagine you're delivering a presentation about the impact of climate change. Instead of starting with dry statistics, you begin with a thought-provoking quote: "The Earth does not belong to us; we belong to the Earth." This introduction immediately engages your audience's emotions and curiosity.

Quote: *"You never get a second chance to make a first impression."* – Will Rogers

Action Plan: Crafting the Perfect Introduction

- ✓ Start with a compelling hook, such as a surprising fact, a relevant quote, a personal anecdote, or a thought-provoking question.
- ✓ Clearly state your main message or thesis to give your audience a roadmap of what to expect.
- ✓ Establish your credibility by briefly mentioning your qualifications or expertise on the topic.

Developing a Clear Main Message

The main message of your presentation is the core idea you want your audience to take away. It's the thread that ties your entire presentation together.

Here's why having a clear main message is essential:

Engaging Example: Imagine you're giving a presentation on time management. Your main message is: "Effective time management is the key to achieving work-life balance." Every point and piece of evidence you present in your speech supports this central idea.

Quote: *"A good speech should be like a woman's skirt: long enough to cover the subject and short enough to create interest."* – Winston Churchill

Action Plan: Crafting a Clear Main Message
- ✓ Clearly define the main message of your presentation in one concise sentence.
- ✓ Ensure that every point, example, and piece of evidence in your presentation supports and reinforces your main message.
- ✓ Continually refer back to your main message throughout your presentation to keep your audience focused.

Creating a Memorable Conclusion

The conclusion of your presentation is your last chance to leave a lasting impression on your audience. It should reinforce your main message and provide a sense of closure. Here's why a memorable conclusion matters:

Engaging Example: Think of a powerful movie ending that leaves you with a sense of awe and satisfaction. Your presentation's conclusion should have a similar impact, leaving your audience with a sense of understanding and inspiration.

Quote: *"The last impression is equally as important as the first."* – Anonymous

Action Plan: Crafting an Impactful Conclusion

✓ Summarize the key points of your presentation, emphasizing how they support your main message.
✓ End with a memorable closing statement, such as a call to action, a thought-provoking quote, or a powerful anecdote.
✓ Reiterate your main message and leave your audience with a clear takeaway.

By following these steps and utilizing examples and quotes, students can create presentations that are engaging, coherent, and impactful.

The Art of Storytelling

This chapter teaches students the art of storytelling, helping them understand why stories are powerful, how to use storytelling techniques effectively, and the impact of incorporating personal anecdotes.

Why Stories Matter

Stories are the backbone of effective communication. They have the power to engage, persuade, and inspire. Here's why stories matter:

Engaging Example: Imagine you're giving a presentation on the importance of teamwork. You could present a list of statistics and theories, or you could share a story about a group of individuals who overcame adversity through teamwork. The latter is more likely to resonate with your audience.

Quote: *"There is no greater agony than bearing an untold story inside you."* – Maya Angelou

Action Plan: Embracing the Power of Stories

- ✓ Identify situations in which stories can enhance your message. Think about past experiences, anecdotes, or real-life examples that relate to your topic.
- ✓ Analyze the emotional impact of different stories and choose the ones that align with your message and audience.
- ✓ Practice storytelling by sharing stories with friends or colleagues to gauge their effectiveness and gather feedback.

Storytelling Techniques

Effective storytelling involves more than just sharing an interesting narrative. It requires using techniques to engage the audience and convey your message effectively. Here's why storytelling techniques are essential:

Engaging Example: Picture a TED Talk where the speaker takes you on a journey, using vivid descriptions, suspense, and relatable characters. Storytelling techniques make the content memorable and impactful.

Quote: *"Stories are how we think. They are how we make meaning of life."* – Pamela Rutledge

Action Plan: Mastering Storytelling Techniques

- ✓ Start with a clear beginning, middle, and end structure for your story. Create a narrative arc that builds tension and leads to a resolution.
- ✓ Use descriptive language to paint a vivid picture in the minds of your audience. Engage their senses by describing sights, sounds, smells, and emotions.
- ✓ Incorporate dialogue and character development to make your story relatable and compelling.

Incorporating Personal Anecdotes

Personal anecdotes are a powerful tool for making your message relatable and authentic. Here's why incorporating personal anecdotes is effective:

Engaging Example: Imagine you're giving a presentation on overcoming adversity. Sharing a personal story of how you faced and conquered a significant challenge adds credibility and emotional resonance to your message.

Quote: *"The most personal is the most creative."* – Martin Scorsese

Action Plan: Sharing Personal Anecdotes

✓ Reflect on your life experiences and identify anecdotes that relate to your message or topic.
✓ Craft your personal stories to fit the context of your presentation, emphasizing the lessons learned or insights gained.
✓ Practice delivering your anecdotes with authenticity and emotion, connecting them to your main message.

By following these steps and utilizing examples and quotes, students can captivate their audience and make their messages memorable and meaningful.

Sample Speech Outline

Here's a sample speech outline for a persuasive presentation on the topic "The Importance of Recycling":

Title: The Importance of Recycling

Introduction

- ✓ Attention-grabber: Start with a startling statistic or a thought-provoking question.
- ✓ Example: "Did you know that every year, over 8 million tons of plastic end up in our oceans?"
- ✓ Introduce the topic and its relevance: Explain why recycling is a critical issue today.
- ✓ State the purpose and thesis: Clearly state your goal and what you intend to persuade your audience of.
- ✓ Example: "Today, I will persuade you that recycling is not just an environmental duty but a necessity for our planet's survival."

Body

I. The Environmental Impact of Recycling

Sub-point 1: Reduction of waste in landfills

- ✓ Supporting facts and statistics: Provide data on the amount of waste generated and how recycling reduces it.
- ✓ Example: "Recycling can divert up to 75% of waste from landfills, reducing the strain on our limited landfill space."

Sub-point 2: Conservation of resources

- ✓ Supporting examples: Explain how recycling conserves valuable resources like trees, water, and energy.
- ✓ Example: "By recycling one ton of paper, we save 17 trees and 7,000 gallons of water."

Sub-point 3: Reduction in greenhouse gas emissions
- ✓ Supporting evidence: Discuss how recycling helps lower carbon emissions.
- ✓ Example: "Recycling aluminum cans saves 95% of the energy required to make the same amount from raw materials."

II. Economic Benefits of Recycling

Sub-point 1: Job creation and economic growth
- ✓ Supporting statistics: Share data on the number of jobs created by recycling industries.
- ✓ Example: "Recycling creates 1.1 million jobs in the United States and contributes $36 billion to the GDP."

Sub-point 2: Cost savings for municipalities
- ✓ Supporting examples: Explain how recycling reduces disposal costs for local governments.
- ✓ Example: "Cities that embrace recycling can save millions of dollars in landfill fees and waste collection."

Sub-point 3: Market demand for recycled materials
- ✓ Supporting trends: Discuss the increasing demand for recycled products.
- ✓ Example: "Consumers are increasingly choosing products made from recycled materials, driving market growth."

III. Individual Responsibility and Action

Sub-point 1: Raising awareness
- ✓ Supporting strategies: Explain how individuals can raise awareness about recycling.
- ✓ Example: "Share information on social media, participate in local clean-up events, and encourage friends and family to recycle."

Sub-point 2: Incorporating recycling into daily life
- ✓ Supporting tips: Provide practical steps for people to recycle in their daily routines.

✓ Example: "Set up recycling bins at home, properly sort recyclables, and support businesses that promote recycling."

Sub-point 3: Advocating for policy changes

✓ Supporting actions: Encourage your audience to advocate for recycling-friendly policies.

✓ Example: "Write to your local representatives, join environmental organizations, and vote for candidates who prioritize recycling."

Conclusion

✓ Summarize key points: Recap the main arguments presented in the speech.

✓ Restate thesis: Remind the audience of the importance of recycling.

✓ Call to action: Encourage your audience to take action or change their behavior.

✓ Example: "Let's work together to reduce waste, conserve resources, and build a sustainable future for generations to come."

This sample speech outline provides a structured framework for a persuasive presentation on recycling. Adapt it to your specific topic and audience to create a compelling and organized speech.

Visual Aids and Multimedia

This section will equip students with the knowledge and skills needed to effectively utilize visual aids and multimedia tools in their presentations.

Selecting and Designing Visuals

Visual aids play a crucial role in enhancing the clarity and impact of your presentations. Here's why selecting and designing visuals is important:

Engaging Example: Imagine you're giving a presentation about wildlife conservation. Instead of a dense slide filled with text, you display a powerful image of a majestic tiger in the wild. This visual instantly captures your audience's attention and reinforces your message.

Quote: *"Design is not just what it looks like and feels like. Design is how it works."* – Steve Jobs

Action Plan: Effective Visual Design

- ✓ Determine the key points or messages you want to convey in your presentation.
- ✓ Select visuals (such as images, charts, graphs, or videos) that align with your content and help illustrate your points.
- ✓ Design visuals that are clear, uncluttered, and visually appealing. Use tools like Canva or PowerPoint to create or enhance visuals.

Using PowerPoint and Other Presentation Tools

PowerPoint and similar tools are valuable aids for organizing and delivering presentations. However, they should enhance, not distract from, your message. Here's why using these tools effectively is crucial:

Engaging Example: Consider a TED Talk by a scientist who uses PowerPoint to showcase stunning images of distant galaxies while explaining complex astrophysical concepts. The visuals enhance the audience's understanding and engagement.

Quote: *"The only thing worse than death by PowerPoint is life by PowerPoint."* – Peter Norvig

Action Plan: Maximizing Presentation Tools
- ✓ Familiarize yourself with the features of your presentation software (e.g., PowerPoint, Google Slides) and practice creating slides.
- ✓ Use a consistent and visually appealing template or theme that aligns with your message and audience.
- ✓ Keep slides concise, using bullet points or brief phrases rather than lengthy paragraphs.

Avoiding Overloaded Slides

One common pitfall in presentations is overcrowded slides filled with excessive text or complex visuals. Avoiding overloaded slides is essential for maintaining audience engagement. Here's why it's crucial:

Engaging Example: Imagine you're attending a lecture, and the presenter displays a slide with tiny font and dense text. It's overwhelming and challenging to follow. In contrast, a slide with minimal text and clear visuals is more engaging and effective.

Quote: *"Simplicity is the ultimate sophistication."* – Leonardo da Vinci

Action Plan: Simplifying Your Slides
- ✓ Limit each slide to one main point or concept. Avoid the temptation to overcrowd it with information.

✓ Use visuals, such as images, diagrams, or infographics, to complement your text and make your message more memorable.
✓ Practice your presentation with a focus on delivering content, not reading directly from the slides.

By following these steps and utilizing examples and quotes, students can create visually appealing, informative, and engaging presentations that enhance their communication efforts.

Tips for Effective Visual Design

Here are some detailed tips for effective visual design:

1. Keep it Simple:
Avoid clutter and visual noise. Simplicity enhances clarity and comprehension. Stick to the essentials.

2. Consistency is Key:
Maintain a consistent design theme throughout your presentation. Use the same fonts, colors, and layouts to create a cohesive look.

3. Use High-Quality Images:
If you use images, ensure they are high-resolution and relevant to your content. Low-quality visuals can detract from your message.

4. Choose Appropriate Fonts:
Select readable fonts that complement your topic and audience. Sans-serif fonts like Arial or Calibri are often easy to read in presentations.

5. Limit Text on Slides:
Avoid lengthy paragraphs. Use concise bullet points or headlines to convey key information. Slides are not meant for reading; they support your spoken words.

6. Use Contrast for Readability:
Ensure text contrasts with the background. Dark text on a light background or vice versa enhances readability.

7. Visual Hierarchy:
Use font size, color, and positioning to create a visual hierarchy. Important points should stand out.

8. Incorporate White Space:

White space (or negative space) helps prevent visual clutter and gives your content room to breathe. It enhances comprehension.

9. Limit Animations and Transitions:
While animations and transitions can be engaging, don't overdo them. Use them sparingly to avoid distractions.

10. Align Elements: Ensure text and visual elements are aligned correctly. Misalignment can create a disorganized look.

11. Use Graphs and Charts Wisely:
When presenting data, use graphs and charts to make complex information more understandable. Label and explain them clearly.

12. Mind Color Psychology:
Be aware of the psychological impact of colors. For example, blue can convey trust and stability, while red can evoke urgency or passion.

13. Accessibility Considerations:
Ensure your visuals are accessible to all audiences. Use high contrast for text, provide alternative text for images, and consider color blindness.

14. Test on Different Screens:
Your presentation may look different on various screens. Test it on multiple devices and adjust as needed.

15. Storytelling Through Visuals:
Visuals should enhance your narrative. Use images, diagrams, and illustrations to tell a story and support your message.

16. Rehearse with Slides:
Practice your presentation with your slides to ensure a seamless flow. This helps you sync your spoken words with visual cues.

17. Seek Feedback:

Before your presentation, get feedback on your visual design from colleagues or mentors. Fresh perspectives can reveal improvements.

18. Keep File Sizes Manageable:

Large file sizes can cause technical issues when sharing your presentation. Compress images and keep multimedia elements optimized.

19. Responsive Design:

If your presentation will be viewed on various devices, consider responsive design principles to ensure it looks good on different screens.

20. Use Templates Wisely:

Templates can be helpful, but don't be overly reliant on them. Customize templates to suit your content and style.

Effective visual design enhances the impact of your presentations and aids in conveying your message. These tips can help you create engaging, informative, and visually appealing slides for your audience.

Body Language and Nonverbal Communication

In this chapter students will be empowered to harness the power of body language and nonverbal communication to enhance their presentations.

The Importance of Body Language

Body language is a powerful form of communication that often speaks louder than words. Understanding its significance is essential for effective presentations. Here's why:

Engaging Example: Imagine two speakers delivering the same message about enthusiasm. Speaker A stands tall, smiles, and uses expressive gestures, while Speaker B slouches, avoids eye contact, and appears disinterested. The audience is more likely to be drawn to Speaker A's positive body language.

Quote: *"The body says what words cannot."* – Martha Graham

Action Plan: Recognizing the Impact of Body Language

- ✓ Record a short video of yourself discussing a topic or giving a practice presentation.
- ✓ Review the video and make note of your body language cues, such as posture, gestures, and facial expressions.
- ✓ Reflect on how your body language aligns with your message and the impression it conveys.

Tips for Effective Gestures and Posture

Gestures and posture are key components of body language that can either enhance or detract from your message. Here's why mastering these aspects is crucial:

Engaging Example: Picture a motivational speaker who uses dynamic hand gestures and maintains an upright posture while discussing achieving goals. These nonverbal cues reinforce their message of confidence and determination.

Quote: *"Your body communicates as powerfully as your words."* – John C. Maxwell

Action Plan: Mastering Gestures and Posture
- ✓ Practice standing or sitting with good posture. Keep your back straight, shoulders relaxed, and head level.
- ✓ Experiment with purposeful gestures that complement your words and emphasize key points in your presentation.
- ✓ Seek feedback from a friend or colleague about your posture and gestures during a practice presentation.

Eye Contact and Facial Expressions

Eye contact and facial expressions are powerful tools for conveying emotions, establishing trust, and connecting with your audience. Here's why they are essential:

Engaging Example: Imagine a speaker who maintains steady eye contact with the audience, smiles when appropriate, and expresses empathy through their facial expressions. This speaker creates a sense of rapport and engagement with the audience.

Quote: *"The eyes indicate the antiquity of the soul."* – Ralph Waldo Emerson

Action Plan: Enhancing Eye Contact and Facial Expressions
- ✓ Practice making eye contact with individuals in your audience. Try to maintain eye contact for

a few seconds before moving on to the next person.

✓ Use a mirror to practice different facial expressions that convey emotions relevant to your message, such as excitement, empathy, or seriousness.

✓ Record a video of yourself giving a presentation, paying special attention to your eye contact and facial expressions. Make adjustments based on your observations.

By following these steps and utilizing examples and quotes, students can develop a compelling and impactful nonverbal communication style that reinforces their verbal message and connects with their audience.

Voice Modulation and Delivery

Students will now be empowered to harness the power of their voices to deliver presentations that are engaging, expressive, and impactful.

The Power of Voice

The way you use your voice can greatly impact the effectiveness of your presentation. Your voice carries the emotional weight of your message and helps you connect with your audience. Here's why understanding the power of your voice is essential:

Engaging Example: Imagine listening to a podcast where the host speaks in a monotone voice throughout. Now, picture another podcast with a host who varies their tone, pitch, and pace to match the excitement or seriousness of the content. The latter is more engaging and memorable.

Quote: *"Words mean more than what is set down on paper. It takes the human voice to infuse them with deeper meaning."* – Maya Angelou

Action Plan: Recognizing the Influence of Your Voice

- ✓ Record yourself reading a passage from a book or a segment of your presentation.
- ✓ Listen to the recording and pay attention to the variations in your tone, pitch, and pace.
- ✓ Reflect on how your voice reflects emotions and conveys meaning.

Techniques for Effective Vocal Delivery

Effective vocal delivery involves techniques that help you articulate your words clearly, express emotions authentically, and maintain your audience's attention. Here's why mastering these techniques matters:

Engaging Example: Picture a charismatic public speaker who captivates the audience with the power and clarity of their voice. They use techniques like modulation, emphasis, and pauses to convey their message persuasively.

Quote: *"Your voice is your tool and your instrument. Cultivate it, nourish it, and never take it for granted."* – Anonymous

Action Plan: Enhancing Vocal Techniques

✓ Practice articulation exercises to improve your diction and pronunciation. Tongue twisters and vocal warm-up routines can help.

✓ Experiment with emphasis and modulation to convey different emotions through your voice. Practice reading passages with different emotional tones.

✓ Use pauses strategically to give your audience time to process information and to emphasize key points.

Practicing Pitch, Pace, and Volume

The pitch, pace, and volume of your voice can be adjusted to match the content, mood, and audience of your presentation. Here's why practicing these aspects is crucial:

Engaging Example: Consider a teacher who lowers their voice to a whisper when sharing a thrilling ghost story with their students. The change in pitch and volume adds suspense and engages the students' imaginations.

Quote: *"You can have the best content in the world, but it doesn't mean anything if your voice isn't engaging."* – Roger Love

Action Plan: Fine-Tuning Pitch, Pace, and Volume

- ✓ Practice delivering a portion of your presentation multiple times, each with a different pitch, pace, or volume to convey different emotions or emphasize different points.
- ✓ Use your voice to match the mood of your content. For instance, slow down and lower your voice for serious or reflective moments, and speed up and raise your voice for excitement.
- ✓ Record yourself practicing vocal variations and listen to the recordings to assess their effectiveness.

By following these steps and utilizing examples and quotes, students can develop effective vocal delivery techniques that enhance their communication skills and connect with their audience on a deeper level.

Managing Nervousness and Anxiety

This chapter equips students with a very important topic- the strategies to manage nervousness and anxiety, allowing them to present with confidence and poise.

Recognizing and Addressing Anxiety

Nervousness and anxiety are common before public speaking, but they can be managed effectively. Understanding and addressing these emotions is essential for confident presentations. Here's why:

Engaging Example: Imagine you're about to deliver a presentation to your classmates, and you feel your heart racing, palms sweating, and your mind racing with negative thoughts. Recognizing these signs of anxiety is the first step towards managing them.

Quote: *"Nervousness is the price you pay for being unprepared."* – Fred Astaire

Action Plan: Identifying and Managing Anxiety

- ✓ Before your next presentation, take a few moments to reflect on your feelings. Are you experiencing physical symptoms of anxiety such as trembling, sweating, or a racing heart?
- ✓ Acknowledge your anxiety without judgment. Remember that it's a natural response to a challenging situation.
- ✓ Develop a positive mantra or affirmation to repeat to yourself before and during your presentation, such as "I am well-prepared, and I can do this."

Breathing and Relaxation Exercises
Controlling your breath and practicing relaxation techniques can help calm your nerves and improve your overall performance. Here's why mastering these techniques is essential:
Engaging Example: Picture a musician about to perform on stage. Before stepping onto the stage, they take a few deep breaths and visualize a successful performance. These techniques help them stay calm and focused under pressure.
Quote: *"Breathe deeply, until sweet air extinguishes the burn of fear in your lungs and every breath is a beautiful refusal to become anything less than infinite."* – D. Antoinette Foy

Action Plan: Practicing Breath Control and Relaxation
- ✓ Practice deep breathing exercises regularly, such as diaphragmatic breathing. Inhale deeply through your nose for a count of four, hold for four, and exhale for four.
- ✓ Experiment with mindfulness or meditation techniques to help you stay present and reduce anxiety.
- ✓ Before your presentation, take a few minutes to close your eyes, focus on your breath, and visualize a successful and confident performance.

Building Confidence through Preparation
Preparation is one of the most effective ways to combat anxiety. Confidence in your content and delivery can significantly reduce nervousness. Here's why building confidence through preparation is crucial:

Engaging Example: Imagine you've spent weeks researching, practicing, and rehearsing your presentation. You know your material inside out. This level of preparation not only boosts your confidence but also reassures your audience of your expertise.

Quote: *"The only way to do great work is to love what you do. If you haven't found it yet, keep looking. Don't settle."* – Steve Jobs

Action Plan: Preparing Confidently
- ✓ Start preparing well in advance of your presentation date. Break down your preparation into manageable tasks, such as researching, outlining, and practicing.
- ✓ Practice your presentation multiple times, ideally in front of a trusted friend or mentor who can provide constructive feedback.
- ✓ Anticipate potential questions or challenges from your audience and prepare thoughtful responses.

By following these steps and utilizing examples and quotes, students can develop practical skills to address anxiety, stay relaxed, and build confidence through thorough preparation.

Captivating Your Audience

In this section students will be empowered with strategies to captivate their audience, including engaging techniques, audience interaction, humor, visual aids, and creating memorable experiences.

Engaging Techniques and Audience Interaction

Engaging your audience is essential for maintaining their interest and involvement throughout your presentation. Here's why engaging techniques and audience interaction matter:

Engaging Example: Imagine a motivational speaker who asks the audience thought-provoking questions, encourages them to share personal experiences, and invites volunteers to participate in interactive activities. The audience becomes active participants rather than passive listeners.

Quote: *"Engagement is not about entertaining the audience. It's about creating an environment where they can learn."* – Chip Heath

Action Plan: Engaging Your Audience

✓ Start your presentation with a compelling story, question, or relevant anecdote to capture your audience's attention.

✓ Incorporate interactive elements, such as polls, discussions, or small group activities, to encourage audience participation.

✓ Encourage questions and feedback throughout your presentation, creating a dynamic dialogue with your audience.

Using Humor and Visual Aids Effectively
Humor and visual aids can enhance the impact of your presentation when used judiciously. Here's why using humor and visuals effectively matters:
Engaging Example: Consider a TED Talk speaker who uses humor to lighten the mood and connect with the audience before delving into a complex scientific topic. Well-timed humor makes the content more approachable and memorable.
Quote: *"Humor is the universal solvent against the abrasive elements of life."* – Stanislaw Jerzy Lec
Action Plan: Leveraging Humor and Visual Aids
- ✓ Incorporate relevant humor that aligns with your message and audience. Avoid offensive or potentially divisive jokes.
- ✓ Utilize visual aids, such as images, videos, or infographics, that enhance understanding and reinforce key points.
- ✓ Practice the timing of humor and visual aids to ensure they complement your presentation without overshadowing your message.

Creating Memorable Experiences
A memorable presentation goes beyond the content; it leaves a lasting impact on your audience. Here's why creating memorable experiences is crucial:
Engaging Example: Imagine attending a conference where a speaker brings in live demonstrations, hands-on activities, or virtual reality experiences related to their topic. These immersive elements transform the presentation into an unforgettable event.
Quote: *"People may forget what you said, but they will never forget how you made them feel."* – Maya Angelou

Action Plan: Crafting Memorable Experiences
- ✓ Identify opportunities to incorporate unique elements into your presentation that align with your message and audience.
- ✓ Consider storytelling techniques that create emotional connections between your audience and your content.
- ✓ Seek feedback from audience members after your presentation to learn what aspects left the most significant impression and adjust your future presentations accordingly.

By following these steps and utilizing examples and quotes, students can create presentations that resonate with their audience and leave a lasting impact.

Handling Q&A Sessions and Feedback

We will now get into equipping students with the knowledge and skills needed to handle Q&A sessions effectively, address challenging questions with confidence, and use feedback as a tool for growth.

Preparing for Questions

The Q&A session is an integral part of any presentation, and being prepared to handle questions effectively is essential. Here's why preparation is crucial:

Engaging Example: Imagine you've just delivered a presentation on a controversial topic. During the Q&A session, an audience member asks a challenging question. Your ability to provide a well-thought-out response demonstrates your expertise and credibility.

Quote: *"The art and science of asking questions is the source of all knowledge."* – Thomas Berger

Action Plan: Preparing for Questions

- ✓ Anticipate potential questions your audience may ask based on your presentation content.
- ✓ Prepare concise and clear answers to these questions. You can create a list of frequently asked questions (FAQs) to guide your preparation.
- ✓ Practice answering questions with a colleague or friend to simulate the Q&A session and receive feedback on your responses.

Dealing with Challenging Questions

Not all questions will be easy to answer, and some may be challenging or critical. Handling such questions gracefully is a valuable skill. Here's why addressing challenging questions matters:

Engaging Example: Picture a politician facing a hostile question during a public debate. Instead of becoming defensive, they respond with composure, addressing the concerns of both the questioner and the broader audience. This skill can turn a potentially negative situation into a moment of credibility and influence.

Quote: *"The best way to escape from a problem is to solve it."* – Alan Saporta

Action Plan: Handling Challenging Questions

- ✓ Maintain composure and actively listen to the question. Take a moment to think before responding.
- ✓ Acknowledge the questioner's perspective and concerns, even if you disagree.
- ✓ Respond with facts, evidence, and a calm demeanor. Avoid becoming defensive or confrontational.

Receiving and Utilizing Feedback

Feedback is a valuable resource for improving your presentation skills. Embracing feedback, whether positive or constructive, can help you grow as a speaker. Here's why feedback is essential:

Engaging Example: Think of a professional athlete who continually seeks feedback from coaches and teammates to refine their skills. Embracing feedback leads to continuous improvement.

Quote: *"Feedback is the breakfast of champions."* – Ken Blanchard

Action Plan: Receiving and Utilizing Feedback
- ✓ Encourage your audience to provide feedback after your presentation. You can use anonymous surveys or open discussions.
- ✓ Analyze the feedback you receive, identifying both strengths and areas for improvement.
- ✓ Develop an action plan to address the feedback. Set specific goals and strategies for enhancing your presentation skills.

By following these steps and utilizing examples and quotes, students can become more adept at engaging with their audience and continuously improving their presentation skills.

Rehearsal and Preparation

This chapter will help and empower students with strategies for effective rehearsal, timing, pacing, and preparation for unexpected situations.

Structured Rehearsal Strategies

Effective rehearsal is key to a successful presentation. Structured rehearsal strategies help you refine your content, improve your delivery, and build confidence. Here's why structured rehearsal matters:

Engaging Example: Imagine you're an actor preparing for a challenging role in a play. Through rigorous rehearsal, you learn your lines, blocking, and cues. The same structured approach can be applied to presentations to ensure a polished performance.

Quote: *"Success is the result of perfection, hard work, learning from failure, loyalty, and persistence."* – Colin Powell

Action Plan: Structured Rehearsal
- ✓ Break down your presentation into manageable sections or key points.
- ✓ Practice each section separately, focusing on your content, vocal delivery, and body language.
- ✓ Gradually integrate sections and rehearse the entire presentation, paying attention to transitions between points.

Timing and Pacing

Maintaining proper timing and pacing during your presentation is essential to keep your audience

engaged and ensure you cover all your points.
Here's why timing and pacing are crucial:
Engaging Example: Picture a storyteller who rushes through a captivating narrative, leaving the audience feeling unsatisfied. Conversely, a well-paced storyteller takes the time to build tension and create a memorable experience.
Quote: *"Pacing and timing are the secrets of life."* – Gary Frank

Action Plan: Timing and Pacing Practice
- ✓ Time yourself during rehearsal to ensure you stay within your allocated presentation time.
- ✓ Use natural pauses, breaths, and transitional phrases to control the pacing of your speech.
- ✓ Practice adjusting your pace to match the content, slowing down for important points and speeding up for less critical information.

Preparing for Unexpected Situations
No presentation goes perfectly according to plan, and being prepared for unexpected situations is crucial for maintaining composure and professionalism. Here's why preparation for the unexpected matters:
Engaging Example: Imagine you're giving a presentation, and the projector suddenly malfunctions, or an unexpected interruption occurs. Your ability to handle such situations with grace and adaptability reflects positively on your presentation skills.
Quote: *"The best preparation for tomorrow is doing your best today."* – H. Jackson Brown Jr.
Action Plan: Preparing for the Unexpected

✓ Consider potential technical issues, interruptions, or challenging questions that could arise during your presentation.
✓ Develop contingency plans or solutions for each possible scenario. For technical issues, have backup materials or alternate ways to convey your message.
✓ Maintain a flexible mindset and adapt to unexpected situations with professionalism and confidence.

By following these steps and utilizing examples and quotes, students can develop a disciplined approach to presentation preparation, ensuring their readiness and poise in any presentation scenario.

The Power of Practice

This chapter underscores the power of practice in honing presentation skills.

Establishing a Practice Routine

Regular practice is the cornerstone of presentation excellence. A structured practice routine helps you refine your skills and build confidence over time. Here's why establishing a practice routine is crucial:

Engaging Example: Think of a professional musician who dedicates hours each day to practice scales, melodies, and techniques. Consistent practice allows them to perform effortlessly and with precision during concerts.

Quote: *"Practice does not make perfect. Only perfect practice makes perfect."* – Vince Lombardi

Action Plan: Building a Practice Routine

- ✓ Set aside dedicated practice time in your schedule. Consistency is key, so aim for daily or weekly practice sessions.
- ✓ Break down your presentation into manageable segments and focus on one aspect at a time, such as content, vocal delivery, or body language.
- ✓ Track your progress by setting specific practice goals and monitoring your improvement over time.

Peer Evaluation and Feedback

Feedback from peers provides valuable insights and helps you identify areas for improvement that you may overlook. Here's why seeking peer evaluation and feedback is essential:

Engaging Example: Consider a public speaking class where students regularly peer-review each other's presentations. These evaluations offer diverse perspectives and constructive feedback that benefit the entire class's growth.

Quote: *"Feedback is the breakfast of champions."* – Ken Blanchard

Action Plan: Seeking Peer Evaluation and Feedback

- ✓ Practice your presentation in front of a trusted friend, colleague, or classmate.
- ✓ Ask your peer to provide specific feedback based on predefined criteria, such as clarity, engagement, and delivery.
- ✓ Use the feedback to identify areas for improvement and adjust your practice sessions accordingly.

Video Recording and Self-Reflection

Video recording allows you to observe yourself objectively, identify areas of improvement, and track your progress. Here's why using video recording and self-reflection is crucial:

Engaging Example: Imagine recording your presentation and noticing that you frequently use filler words like "um" and "uh." Recognizing this habit prompts you to focus on reducing such distractions during your practice.

Quote: *"The mirror reflects all objects without being sullied."* – Confucius

Action Plan: Utilizing Video Recording and Self-Reflection

- ✓ Record yourself delivering your presentation in a realistic setting, such as the room where you will present.

- ✓ Watch the recording with a critical eye, paying attention to aspects like body language, vocal delivery, and content organization.
- ✓ Identify specific areas that need improvement and create an action plan to address them in subsequent practice sessions.

By establishing a practice routine, seeking peer evaluation and feedback, and using video recording for self-reflection, students can systematically improve their abilities and build confidence in their presentation delivery.

Overcoming Common Pitfalls

In this section students will be equipped with strategies to overcome common presentation pitfalls, handle technical issues, and recover gracefully from mistakes.

Avoiding Common Presentation Mistakes

Presentation mistakes are common but avoidable with awareness and preparation. Recognizing these pitfalls is the first step to sidestepping them. Here's why avoiding common mistakes is crucial:

Engaging Example: Imagine a presenter who continuously fumbles with their notes, loses their train of thought, and uses too much jargon. These common mistakes can detract from the overall message and weaken the presentation's impact.

Quote: *"To err is human, but when the eraser wears out ahead of the pencil, you're overdoing it."* – Josh Jenkins

Action Plan: Avoiding Common Mistakes
- ✓ Identify the common mistakes related to presentations, such as using filler words (e.g., "um," "uh"), reading slides verbatim, or speaking too quickly.
- ✓ Create a checklist of these mistakes and use it as a reference during your rehearsal and actual presentation.
- ✓ Record yourself during practice presentations to identify and correct recurring mistakes.

Handling Technical Issues

Technical issues can disrupt even the most well-prepared presentations. Knowing how to address these issues can prevent them from derailing your message. Here's why handling technical issues is essential:

Engaging Example: Picture a speaker whose microphone suddenly stops working during a conference presentation. Instead of panicking, they seamlessly switch to a handheld microphone provided by the AV team, ensuring their message is uninterrupted.

Quote: *"The show must go on."* – Proverb

Action Plan: Managing Technical Issues

- ✓ Familiarize yourself with the presentation equipment and software you'll be using, including backup options in case of failure.
- ✓ Before your presentation, arrive early to test all technical aspects, such as microphones, projectors, and slides.
- ✓ Have a contingency plan ready, such as printed materials or alternate ways to convey your message, in case of major technical failures.

Recovering from Mistakes

Mistakes are a part of public speaking, but your ability to recover gracefully can make all the difference. Here's why knowing how to recover from mistakes is crucial:

Engaging Example: Imagine you misspeak a critical statistic during your presentation. Instead of dwelling on the error, you quickly correct yourself, apologize for any confusion, and continue confidently. Your audience appreciates your transparency and professionalism.

Quote: *"Success is not final, failure is not fatal: It is the courage to continue that counts."* – Winston Churchill

Action Plan: Recovering from Mistakes
- ✓ When you make a mistake, pause briefly to collect your thoughts and acknowledge the error calmly.
- ✓ Correct the mistake, providing the accurate information or clarification.
- ✓ Continue your presentation without dwelling on the mistake, focusing on the message ahead.

By following these steps and utilizing examples and quotes, students can approach their presentations with confidence, resilience, and professionalism, ensuring a smoother and more impactful delivery.

Assessment after Reading and Practicing

Assess Yourself: Self-Evaluation of Improved Presentation Skills

These assessment formats will help you gauge your progress and identify areas where you have improved after reading and practicing the principles from the book.

It's essential to be honest with yourself and open to feedback from others to make the most significant improvements in your presentation skills.

Content Clarity (Scale: 1-5)
- ✓ Reassess your ability to communicate ideas and messages clearly after applying the principles from the book.
- ✓ 1 = No improvement, 5 = Significant improvement.

Confidence Level (Scale: 1-5)
- ✓ Evaluate whether your confidence in presenting has increased after practicing the book's principles.
- ✓ 1 = No improvement, 5 = Significant improvement.

Audience Engagement (Scale: 1-5)
- ✓ Rate your effectiveness at engaging the audience following your practice.
- ✓ 1 = No improvement, 5 = Significant improvement.

Use of Visual Aids (Scale: 1-5)
- ✓ Assess whether your proficiency in using visual aids has improved.

- ✓ 1 = No improvement, 5 = Significant improvement.

Body Language and Nonverbal Communication (Scale: 1-5)
- ✓ Reevaluate your body language, gestures, and eye contact.
- ✓ 1 = No improvement, 5 = Significant improvement.

Vocal Delivery (Scale: 1-5)
- ✓ Measure the progress in your vocal skills, including pitch, pace, and modulation.
- ✓ 1 = No improvement, 5 = Significant improvement.

Time Management (Scale: 1-5)
- ✓ Evaluate whether you have become better at managing your presentation time.
- ✓ 1 = No improvement, 5 = Significant improvement.

Handling Q&A Sessions (Scale: 1-5)
- ✓ Assess whether you now handle Q&A sessions with more confidence and effectiveness.
- ✓ 1 = No improvement, 5 = Significant improvement.

Overall Presentation Skills (Scale: 1-10)
- ✓ Provide an updated overall rating of your presentation skills after reading and practicing.
- ✓ 1 = No improvement, 10 = Remarkable improvement.

Peer or Instructor Evaluation (Optional)
Seek feedback from peers or instructors to obtain external assessments of your improved presentation skills.

Special Types of Presentations

We will now equip students with strategies to excel in special types of presentations, including group presentations, job interviews, elevator pitches, persuasive speeches, and informative speeches.

Group Presentations and Collaborative Work

Group presentations require effective teamwork and coordination among team members. Understanding how to collaborate and present as a group is essential. Here's why group presentations matter:

Engaging Example: Consider a business team pitching a project proposal to a potential client. Each team member plays a specific role, seamlessly transitioning between presenters, and collectively showcasing their expertise. This demonstrates professionalism and enhances the overall impact of the presentation.

Quote: *"Teamwork is the ability to work together toward a common vision. It is the fuel that allows common people to attain uncommon results."* – Andrew Carnegie

Action Plan: Excelling in Group Presentations

- ✓ Define individual roles and responsibilities within the group, assigning tasks based on each member's strengths and expertise.
- ✓ Develop a clear and cohesive narrative that integrates each team member's contributions seamlessly.
- ✓ Rehearse as a group to ensure smooth transitions, consistent pacing, and a unified presentation style.

Job Interviews and Elevator Pitches

Job interviews and elevator pitches are critical opportunities to showcase your skills and qualifications concisely and persuasively. Here's why excelling in these situations is crucial:

Engaging Example: Imagine you're in an elevator with a potential employer, and they ask, "Tell me about yourself." A well-crafted elevator pitch that highlights your unique strengths and experiences can make a lasting impression.

Quote: *"Your elevator pitch should not only explain what you do—it should also inspire conversation and build deeper connections."* – Anonymous

Action Plan: Mastering Interviews and Elevator Pitches

- ✓ Craft a succinct elevator pitch that introduces yourself, highlights your key skills and achievements, and concludes with a call to action (e.g., expressing interest in a job opportunity).
- ✓ Prepare for common interview questions by practicing your responses, focusing on conveying your qualifications and demonstrating your fit for the role.
- ✓ Engage in mock interviews with peers or mentors to receive feedback on your interview or pitch performance.

Persuasive and Informative Speeches

Persuasive and informative speeches require distinct approaches to effectively convey your message. Understanding how to tailor your content and delivery is essential. Here's why these types of presentations matter:

Engaging Example: Think of a politician delivering a persuasive campaign speech. They use persuasive techniques such as compelling storytelling, emotional appeal, and strong evidence to sway the audience's opinion and garner support.

Quote: *"The power to persuade is the power to succeed."* – Mia Hamm

Action Plan: Excelling in Persuasive and Informative Speeches

- ✓ Define the purpose and objective of your speech. Are you aiming to inform, persuade, or both?
- ✓ Organize your content according to the specific goals of your speech. Use clear, structured outlines for informative presentations and persuasive techniques (e.g., ethos, pathos, logos) for persuasive ones.
- ✓ Practice delivery techniques that align with your speech type. For persuasive speeches, focus on building emotional connections and using rhetorical devices effectively. For informative speeches, prioritize clarity and the effective transfer of information.

By following these steps and utilizing examples and quotes, students can adapt their presentation skills to various contexts, showcasing their abilities and achieving their goals effectively.

25 Do's of a Great Presentation

Remember, a great presentation is a balance of preparation, engagement, and effective communication. Following these do's and avoiding the don'ts in the next section will help you become a more confident and influential presenter.

1. Know Your Audience:
   Do: Understand your audience's background, interests, and expectations to tailor your content accordingly.
   Example: If you're presenting to a class, consider your peers' prior knowledge and adapt your explanations accordingly.

2. Practice, Practice, Practice:
   Do: Rehearse your presentation multiple times to build confidence and ensure a smooth delivery.
   Example: Athletes practice tirelessly before a big game; similarly, speakers should rehearse before their presentations.

3. Start with a Strong Hook:
   Do: Begin with a compelling story, quote, question, or surprising fact to grab your audience's attention.
   Example: "Imagine a world without smartphones. Would you believe that just two decades ago, it was our reality?"

4. Organize Your Content:
   Do: Structure your presentation with a clear introduction, main points, and conclusion.
   Example: Use a logical order like chronological, problem-solution, or cause-effect to guide your audience.

5. Use Visuals Wisely:
   Do: Incorporate relevant visuals (images, graphs, slides) to enhance understanding and engagement.
   Example: Include a graph to illustrate the growth of a company's revenue over the past five years.
6. Tell Stories:
   Do: Use storytelling to connect with your audience emotionally and make your content memorable.
   Example: Share a personal experience related to your topic to humanize your message.
7. Engage Your Audience:
   Do: Encourage participation through questions, polls, or interactive activities.
   Example: Ask the audience for their opinions on a current issue and invite them to share their thoughts.
8. Maintain Eye Contact:
   Do: Establish a connection with your audience by looking at them, making eye contact, and scanning the room.
   Example: Divide your audience into sections and connect with individuals in each section.
9. Speak Clearly and Slowly:
   Do: Articulate your words, and pace your speech to ensure everyone can follow along.
   Example: Enunciate each syllable, especially when presenting complex terms.
10. Use Gestures and Body Language:
    Do: Utilize natural gestures and body language to emphasize points and express enthusiasm.

Example: When discussing growth, open your arms wide to signify expansion.

11. Practice Vocal Variety:

    Do: Vary your pitch, pace, and tone to keep your audience engaged.

    Example: Use a lower, slower voice for serious topics and a higher, faster voice for excitement.

12. Stay Positive and Confident:

    Do: Exude confidence and maintain a positive attitude, even if you encounter challenges.

    Example: Smile and maintain composure if you make a minor mistake.

13. Address Counterarguments:

    Do: Anticipate potential objections or counterarguments and address them to strengthen your position.

    Example: "Some may argue that, but let me explain why our approach is more effective."

14. Cite Sources and Give Credit:

    Do: Provide proper attribution for facts, statistics, or ideas that are not your own.

    Example: "According to a study published in [Source],..."

15. Be Mindful of Time:

    Do: Respect your allotted time and stay within your presentation's time limit.

    Example: Set a timer during rehearsals to ensure you adhere to the schedule.

16. Invite Questions:

    Do: Encourage questions and discussions at appropriate times during your presentation.

    Example: "Feel free to interrupt with questions, or we can address them at the end."

17. Summarize Key Points:
    Do: Recap your main points at the end to reinforce the core message.
    Example: "In summary, we've discussed three key strategies for sustainable business growth."
18. Use Transition Phrases:
    Do: Employ transition phrases (e.g., "moving on," "next," "in conclusion") to guide your audience smoothly between sections.
    Example: "Now that we've covered the background, let's delve into our solutions."
19. Adapt to Technical Glitches:
    Do: Prepare for technical issues by having a backup plan or alternative presentation formats.
    Example: If your slides fail, be ready to switch to a verbal explanation.
20. Dress Appropriately:
    Do: Choose attire that suits the occasion and reflects professionalism.
    Example: Wear business attire for formal presentations but opt for smart casual for informal settings.
21. Stay Hydrated:
    Do: Have water on hand to stay hydrated during your presentation.
    Example: Take a sip of water when transitioning between sections to avoid throat dryness.
22. Adapt to Your Environment:
    Do: Familiarize yourself with the presentation space and adapt to its setup.
    Example: Arrange your materials accordingly, considering the room layout.

23. Respect Diverse Perspectives:
    Do: Acknowledge and respect diverse opinions and perspectives within your audience.
    Example: "While we may have different viewpoints, let's explore this topic together."
24. Seek Feedback:
    Do: After your presentation, ask for constructive feedback from peers or mentors to improve your skills.
    Example: "What did you find most effective in my presentation, and where can I improve?"
25. Reflect and Improve:
    Do: After each presentation, reflect on your performance and identify areas for improvement.
    Example: Create an improvement plan, setting specific goals for your next presentation.

25 Don'ts of a Great Presentation

1. Don't Overload Slides:
   Don't: Avoid overcrowding slides with too much text or visuals, as it can overwhelm your audience.
2. Don't Read Slides Verbatim:
   Don't: Never read slides word-for-word; instead, elaborate on the key points to provide context.
3. Don't Memorize Entirely:
   Don't: While practice is essential, avoid rigidly memorizing your entire speech, as it may lead to robotic delivery.
4. Don't Rush Through Content:
   Don't: Resist the urge to rush; speaking too quickly can hinder comprehension.
5. Don't Ignore Time Limits:
   Don't: Respect time constraints; exceeding your allotted time can inconvenience the audience.
6. Don't Be Overly Technical:
   Don't: If your audience lacks expertise in your field, avoid using overly technical jargon without explanation.
7. Don't Use Distractions:
   Don't: Minimize distractions like excessive animations, sound effects, or busy backgrounds in your slides.
8. Don't Neglect Relevance:
   Don't: Ensure all content directly relates to your topic; unrelated tangents can confuse your audience.
9. Don't Be Overly Negative:

Don't: Maintain a positive tone and avoid excessive criticism or negativity.

10. Don't Monopolize the Time:
    Don't: Give other participants an opportunity to speak during group presentations; avoid hogging the spotlight.

11. Don't Ignore Nonverbal Cues:
    Don't: Be attuned to your audience's nonverbal cues, such as body language or expressions, and adjust your approach accordingly.

12. Don't Use Excessive Filler Words:
    Don't: Minimize filler words like "um," "uh," and "like" to sound more polished and confident.

13. Don't Overwhelm with Information:
    Don't: Avoid presenting excessive data or information; focus on the most relevant and impactful points.

14. Don't Lack Clarity:
    Don't: Ensure your message is crystal clear; ambiguity can confuse your audience.

15. Don't Disregard Preparation:
    Don't: Never "wing it"; thorough preparation is essential for a successful presentation.

16. Don't Engage in Controversial Topics Without Consideration:
    Don't: If addressing controversial topics, be mindful of diverse opinions, and foster respectful discussion.

17. Don't Disrespect Time Limits:
    Don't: Avoid ending abruptly or exceeding your time limit, as it can disrupt schedules.

18. Don't Ignore Feedback:

Don't: Don't dismiss feedback, whether positive or negative; it's a valuable tool for improvement.

19. Don't Ramble:
Don't: Stay concise and on-topic; aim to convey your message without excessive elaboration.

20. Don't Neglect the Introduction and Conclusion:
Don't: Don't overlook the importance of a compelling introduction and a memorable conclusion.

21. Don't Lack Enthusiasm:
Don't: Maintain energy and enthusiasm throughout your presentation to engage your audience.

22. Don't Speak in a Monotone:
Don't: Avoid a monotone voice; infuse your speech with vocal variety to captivate your audience.

23. Don't Rely Solely on Text:
Don't: Don't rely exclusively on text-based slides; incorporate visuals and multimedia to enhance understanding.

24. Don't Ignore Cultural Sensitivity:
Don't: Be respectful of cultural differences; avoid humor or references that may be offensive or insensitive.

25. Don't Panic Over Mistakes:
Don't: If you make a mistake, remain composed and continue; panicking draws unnecessary attention.

Building a Personal Brand

This chapter underscores the importance of building a personal brand through public speaking. By crafting your public speaking persona, leveraging public speaking for personal growth, and utilizing it as a networking and career advancement tool, students can enhance their professional identity and create meaningful opportunities for themselves.

Crafting Your Public Speaking Persona

Your public speaking persona is how you present yourself to the world as a speaker. It encompasses your style, values, and the image you project. Here's why crafting your public speaking persona matters:

Engaging Example: Think of a renowned motivational speaker known for their charismatic and energetic delivery. Their persona aligns with their message of positivity and empowerment, making them a sought-after speaker in their field.

Quote: *"Your personal brand is a promise to your clients... a promise of quality, consistency, competency, and reliability."* – Jason Hartman

Action Plan: Defining Your Public Speaking Persona

- ✓ Reflect on your core values, strengths, and the message you want to convey through your presentations.
- ✓ Identify key traits and qualities that define your persona, such as confidence, authenticity, or expertise.
- ✓ Align your persona with your message, ensuring consistency in your delivery and communication style.

Leveraging Public Speaking for Personal Growth
Public speaking offers numerous opportunities for personal growth, including improved communication skills, increased self-confidence, and enhanced self-awareness. Here's why leveraging public speaking for personal growth is important:
Engaging Example: Consider someone who initially had a fear of public speaking but, through consistent practice and dedication, transformed into a confident and articulate speaker. This personal growth not only benefits their career but also their overall self-esteem and well-being.
Quote: *"The only way to do great work is to love what you do."* – Steve Jobs
Action Plan: Using Public Speaking for Personal Growth
- ✓ Set specific personal growth goals related to your public speaking journey, such as improving your confidence, expanding your knowledge, or overcoming specific fears.
- ✓ Seek opportunities for public speaking, whether through workshops, presentations, or volunteering, to continuously challenge and refine your skills.
- ✓ Reflect on your progress and the lessons learned from each speaking engagement, using these insights to fuel your personal growth.

Networking and Career Advancement
Public speaking is a powerful tool for networking and advancing your career. It allows you to connect with like-minded individuals, showcase your expertise, and open doors to new opportunities. Here's why networking and career advancement through public speaking are crucial:

Engaging Example: Imagine attending a conference where you deliver a well-received presentation. Afterward, several attendees approach you to discuss potential collaborations or job opportunities. Your speaking engagements have expanded your professional network and career prospects.

Quote: *"Your network is your net worth."* – Porter Gale

Action Plan: Leveraging Public Speaking for Networking and Career Advancement

- ✓ Identify events, conferences, or organizations related to your field where you can offer your expertise as a speaker.
- ✓ Develop a compelling speaker profile or portfolio showcasing your accomplishments, topics of expertise, and speaking experience.
- ✓ Actively engage with your audience and fellow speakers during events, exchanging contact information and building lasting professional relationships.

Going Beyond the Classroom

In this section, we will emphasize the enduring nature of public speaking skills and their relevance beyond the classroom. By applying these skills in real-life situations, engaging in community leadership, and viewing public speaking as a lifelong skill, students can harness the full potential of their communication abilities to make a lasting impact.

Applying Public Speaking Skills in Real-Life Situations

Public speaking skills extend beyond the classroom and can be applied in various real-life scenarios. Learning how to adapt these skills to different situations is valuable. Here's why applying public speaking skills in real life matters:

Engaging Example: Consider a student who, after mastering public speaking in class, becomes a youth advocate in their community. They use their skills to speak at local events, advocating for positive change and inspiring others.

Quote: *"Real learning comes about when the competitive spirit has ceased."* – Jiddu Krishnamurti

Action Plan: Applying Public Speaking Skills in Real-Life Situations

- ✓ Identify opportunities in your community or personal life where public speaking can be valuable, such as community meetings, volunteer work, or advocacy efforts.
- ✓ Prepare for these situations by tailoring your message to your audience and the context.
- ✓ Reflect on your experiences, noting what worked well and areas for improvement, and

use this feedback to refine your skills for future occasions.

Community Engagement and Leadership
Public speaking plays a vital role in community engagement and leadership. Effective communication can inspire positive change and mobilize others. Here's why community engagement and leadership through public speaking are crucial:
Engaging Example: Think of a community leader who uses public speaking to address important issues, rally support, and motivate residents to take action. Their ability to connect with the community through speeches and presentations is instrumental in driving change.
Quote: *"Leadership is not about being in charge. It is about taking care of those in your charge."* – Simon Sinek
Action Plan: Engaging in Community Leadership through Public Speaking
- ✓ Identify community issues or causes you are passionate about and consider how public speaking can contribute to addressing these concerns.
- ✓ Develop a clear message that resonates with your community and aligns with your goals.
- ✓ Actively engage with community members through public speaking, organizing events, or leading initiatives that promote positive change.

Public Speaking as a Lifelong Skill
Public speaking is not limited to a specific phase of life but is a skill that can be continually honed and

applied throughout one's lifetime. Here's why viewing public speaking as a lifelong skill is essential:

Engaging Example: Imagine an individual who, well into their retirement years, continues to engage in public speaking opportunities, sharing their life experiences and wisdom with younger generations. Their commitment to lifelong learning and communication sets an inspiring example.

Quote: *"Education is the most powerful weapon which you can use to change the world."* – Nelson Mandela

Action Plan: Embracing Public Speaking as a Lifelong Skill

- ✓ Recognize that public speaking is a skill that can benefit you throughout your life, whether personally, professionally, or as a means of sharing your knowledge and experiences.
- ✓ Continuously seek opportunities to refine your public speaking skills, such as attending workshops, joining speaking clubs, or mentoring others.
- ✓ Embrace each new phase of life as an opportunity to adapt and apply your public speaking skills in meaningful ways, contributing to your personal growth and the betterment of your community.

Continuous Improvement and Growth to Becoming a Proficient Speaker

This chapter provides students with guidance on accessing recommended resources, engaging with public speaking organizations and clubs, and fostering a growth mindset for continuous improvement.

Access to valuable resources

The journey to becoming a proficient public speaker involves continuous learning. Access to valuable resources can accelerate your growth. Here's why knowing where to find recommended resources matters:

Engaging Example: Consider a student who wants to improve their storytelling skills. By reading books, enrolling in online courses, and exploring storytelling websites, they enhance their ability to craft engaging narratives for their presentations.

Quote: *"The beautiful thing about learning is that no one can take it away from you."* – B.B. King

Action Plan: Accessing Recommended Resources

- ✓ Research and compile a list of recommended books, online courses, and websites related to public speaking and communication skills.
- ✓ Set aside dedicated time for self-study and exploration of these resources, making it a consistent part of your learning journey.
- ✓ Apply the knowledge gained from these resources to your practice and presentations,

actively integrating new techniques and insights.

Public Speaking Organizations and Clubs
Joining public speaking organizations and clubs provides a supportive community of like-minded individuals and opportunities for practice and networking. Here's why involvement in such groups can be transformative:

Engaging Example: Imagine a student who joins a Toastmasters club. Through regular meetings, speeches, and evaluations, they not only improve their public speaking skills but also develop leadership abilities, gain confidence, and build lasting friendships.

Quote: *"You are the average of the five people you spend the most time with."* – Jim Rohn

Action Plan: Engaging with Public Speaking Organizations and Clubs
- ✓ Research local or online public speaking organizations and clubs that align with your goals and interests.
- ✓ Attend meetings or events to get a sense of the community and offerings.
- ✓ Become an active member by participating in speaking opportunities, taking on leadership roles, and contributing to the group's growth and development.

Continuous Improvement and Growth
Public speaking is a dynamic skill that evolves with practice and self-reflection. Committing to continuous improvement is key to mastery. Here's why fostering a growth mindset in public speaking is essential:

Engaging Example: Think of a seasoned speaker who, despite their accomplishments, remains open to feedback and actively seeks opportunities to enhance their skills. This commitment to growth keeps their presentations fresh and impactful.

Quote: *"The key to pursuing excellence is to embrace an organic, long-term learning process and not live in a shell of static, safe mediocrity."* – Josh Waitzkin

Action Plan: Cultivating Continuous Improvement

- ✓ Set specific goals for your public speaking journey, both short-term and long-term.
- ✓ Regularly evaluate your progress and areas for improvement, seeking feedback from peers, mentors, or audience members.
- ✓ Embrace challenges and stepping out of your comfort zone, taking on new speaking opportunities that stretch your abilities and knowledge.

By following these steps and utilizing examples and quotes, students can navigate their ongoing journey toward becoming confident and effective public speakers.

Gaining from Success Stories and Insights

This part showcases the success stories, journeys, and lessons learned from accomplished speakers and leaders. By incorporating interviews, sharing personal experiences, and distilling valuable insights, this chapter empowers readers with real-world guidance and inspiration to enhance their public speaking skills and confidence.

Interviews with Successful Speakers and Leaders
Learning from the experiences and wisdom of accomplished speakers and leaders can be incredibly inspiring and informative. Here's why including interviews with successful individuals in your book matters:

Engaging Example: Imagine featuring an interview with a renowned TED speaker known for their compelling talks. They share insights into their journey, the challenges they've faced, and their strategies for captivating audiences. Their story resonates with readers, inspiring them to pursue their own speaking goals.

Quote: *"Success is not the key to happiness. Happiness is the key to success. If you love what you are doing, you will be successful."* – Albert Schweitzer

Action Plan: Conducting Interviews with Successful Speakers
✓ Identify accomplished speakers or leaders who can offer valuable insights and inspiration to your readers.

- ✓ Prepare thoughtful and relevant interview questions that delve into their speaking journey, challenges, and strategies.
- ✓ Conduct the interviews, capturing their stories and perspectives in a way that resonates with your readers.

Their Journey to Confidence and Success

Exploring the paths successful speakers have taken to reach their current level of confidence and achievement provides valuable guidance to aspiring speakers. Here's why sharing their journeys is essential:

Engaging Example: Consider a successful speaker who, in their interview, recounts their early struggles with stage fright and self-doubt. They describe the techniques and mindset shifts that gradually transformed them into a confident and effective speaker. Their journey serves as a roadmap for readers facing similar challenges.

Quote: *"Your journey has molded you for your greater good, and it was exactly what it needed to be. Don't think you've lost time. It took each and every situation you have encountered to bring you to the now. And now is right on time."* – Asha Tyson

Action Plan: Sharing Success Stories and Journeys

- ✓ Highlight key turning points and milestones in the journeys of successful speakers and leaders.
- ✓ Emphasize the challenges they faced and the strategies they employed to overcome them.
- ✓ Encourage readers to reflect on their own journey, drawing inspiration from the

experiences of others to overcome obstacles and build confidence.

Lessons Learned from Accomplished Individuals
Extracting valuable lessons and actionable insights from accomplished individuals helps readers apply these principles to their own speaking endeavors. Here's why distilling lessons is important:
Engaging Example: Imagine a successful speaker sharing a lesson on the importance of authenticity in public speaking. They emphasize the impact of genuine, heartfelt communication and offer practical tips for cultivating authenticity in one's presentations.
Quote: *"The only source of knowledge is experience."* – Albert Einstein
Action Plan: Extracting and Applying Lessons
- ✓ Identify key lessons and insights from the interviews and success stories of accomplished individuals.
- ✓ Translate these lessons into actionable steps and strategies that readers can apply to their own speaking journey.
- ✓ Encourage readers to incorporate these lessons into their practice, presentations, and personal growth.

Exercises and Activities for Skill Development

Here are some detailed exercises and activities for skill development in the context of public speaking and presentation skills. These exercises and activities provide a range of opportunities for skill development in public speaking and presentation. Customize them based on the specific needs and objectives of your audience or training program.

1. Impromptu Speaking Practice:
Purpose: Enhance improvisational speaking skills.
Activity: In a group, draw random topics or scenarios from a hat and speak on them for one to two minutes. Encourage each member to think on their feet and organize their thoughts quickly. Provide feedback to one another

2. Peer Feedback Sessions:
Purpose: Improve the ability to give and receive constructive feedback.
Activity: Divide the team into pairs or small groups. Each participant takes turns delivering a short presentation, and the others provide feedback using specific criteria, such as content, delivery, and body language.

3. Elevator Pitch Challenge:
Purpose: Refine concise communication skills.
Activity: Ask each member in the team to craft a 30-second elevator pitch about themselves or a chosen topic. They should practice delivering it to a partner, focusing on clarity and impact.

4. Storytelling Workshops:
Purpose: Develop storytelling abilities.

Activity: Organize storytelling workshops where team members share personal anecdotes or stories related to their experiences. Encourage one another to work on narrative structure, engaging beginnings, and emotional connections.

5. Visual Aid Design Competition:
Purpose: Enhance visual design skills for presentations.
Activity: Give members of the team a topic and ask them to create a single slide or visual aid that effectively conveys the key message. Have a set of Judges that can evaluate for clarity, creativity, and alignment with the topic.

6. Impersonation and Character Building:
Purpose: Encourage versatility in delivery.
Activity: Have members choose a historical figure, famous personality, or fictional character and prepare a short presentation in that character's style. This exercise helps explore different speaking styles.

7. Mock Panel Discussions:
Purpose: Build skills in group communication and debate.
Activity: Form a panel of members who take on different roles and engage in a moderated discussion or debate on a specific topic. This activity enhances teamwork and argumentation skills.

8. Speech Analysis and Critique:
Purpose: Improve critical thinking and analytical skills.
Activity: Have a famous speech or presentation shown to all and have them analyze it. Ask them to identify effective techniques, areas for improvement, and key takeaways.

9. Voice Modulation Exercises:
Purpose: Enhance vocal variety and expressiveness.

Activity: Have members go through exercises that involve varying pitch, pace, and volume while delivering a short passage or story. This helps them understand the impact of voice modulation.

10. Presentation Redesign Challenge:

Purpose: Promote adaptability and revision skills.

Activity: Provide members with a poorly designed presentation and ask them to redesign it for clarity and engagement. This exercise emphasizes the importance of adapting content for different audiences.

11. Panel Role Rotation:

Purpose: Foster adaptability and versatility in panel discussions.

Activity: In a panel discussion setting, periodically rotate members into different roles (e.g., moderator, expert, skeptic) to challenge their ability to adapt to different speaking roles and perspectives.

12. Visualization and Meditation:

Purpose: Reduce nervousness and improve focus.

Activity: Have team members led through visualization and meditation exercises before speaking engagements to help them relax, visualize success, and manage anxiety.

13. Audience Interaction Activities:

Purpose: Encourage engagement with the audience.

Activity: Integrate audience interaction elements into presentations, such as polls, questions, or group discussions. This practice helps speakers connect with their audience.

14. Virtual Presentation Simulation: Purpose: Adapt to virtual presentation environments. Activity: Conduct virtual presentations and simulate online meeting scenarios. Practice sharing screens, managing virtual tools, and maintaining audience engagement.

The Journey to Becoming a Confident Speaker

This chapter encourages students to reflect on their journey, set future goals, and embrace the path to mastery in public speaking.

Reflecting on Your Journey

As students near the conclusion of their journey to becoming confident speakers, it's essential to take a moment for introspection and reflection. Here's why reflecting on their journey is valuable:

Engaging Example: Picture a student who initially struggled with public speaking, but over time, through dedication and practice, transformed into a poised and effective communicator. By looking back at their progress, they gain a sense of accomplishment and motivation for the road ahead.

Quote: *"The unexamined life is not worth living."* – Socrates

Action Plan: Reflecting on Your Speaking Journey

- ✓ Set aside time for quiet reflection on your journey, from your initial challenges to your recent successes.
- ✓ Journal your thoughts and feelings about the progress you've made, the skills you've developed, and the obstacles you've overcome.
- ✓ Celebrate your growth and use this reflection as a source of inspiration for the future.

Setting Goals for Future Growth

Even as confident speakers, there's always room for improvement and new challenges to conquer. Setting goals for future growth keeps the journey exciting and purposeful. Here's why setting goals is essential: Engaging Example: Imagine a student who, having gained confidence in public speaking, now sets their sights on delivering a TED Talk or becoming a mentor to others struggling with stage fright. These ambitious goals drive them to continually refine their skills.

Quote: *"The only thing standing between you and your goal is the story you keep telling yourself as to why you can't achieve it."* – Jordan Belfort

Action Plan: Setting Goals for Future Growth

- ✓ Define specific and measurable goals for your public speaking journey, considering areas of improvement, new challenges, or opportunities you want to explore.
- ✓ Break these goals into smaller, manageable milestones, making it easier to track your progress.
- ✓ Create a timeline for achieving these goals and regularly revisit and adjust them as needed.

The Ongoing Path to Mastery

Public speaking is a skill that can be continually refined and mastered. Encourage students to view their journey as an ongoing path to mastery. Here's why embracing this mindset is crucial:

Engaging Example: Think of a seasoned speaker who, despite their expertise, continues to seek out workshops, mentors, and new speaking opportunities. Their dedication to ongoing growth keeps their skills sharp and presentations impactful.

Quote: *"The more I practice, the luckier I get."* – Gary Player

Action Plan: Embracing the Path to Mastery
- ✓ Acknowledge that public speaking is a skill that can always be improved, regardless of your current level of proficiency.
- ✓ Commit to a lifelong journey of learning, seeking out opportunities for growth, and staying open to feedback and new techniques.
- ✓ Embrace each speaking engagement as a chance to refine your skills and connect with your audience more effectively.

By following these steps and utilizing examples and quotes, students can embark on a lifelong journey of confident and impactful communication.

The Future of Presentations: Thriving in a Digital Age

In an era marked by rapid technological advancements and shifting communication landscapes, the art of presentation has evolved significantly. The traditional boundaries of physical presentations have expanded into the digital realm, creating new opportunities and challenges for communicators. In this chapter, we will explore the future of presentations, equipping you with the knowledge and skills needed to stand out in the digital age.

I. Virtual Presentations and Webinars: The New Norm

In an increasingly remote world, the ability to deliver compelling virtual presentations and webinars is essential. Here's what you should be prepared to work on:

1. Technology Mastery
   - ✓ Familiarize yourself with virtual platforms like Zoom, Microsoft Teams, and Google Meet.
   - ✓ Learn to navigate advanced features such as screen sharing, breakout rooms, and polls.
2. Engaging Content for Online Audiences
   - ✓ Craft presentations optimized for online consumption, using concise visuals and interactive elements.
   - ✓ Incorporate audience engagement tools like live chat, Q&A sessions, and virtual whiteboards.
3. Overcoming Virtual Challenges

- ✓ Develop strategies to combat common virtual presentation challenges like distractions and technical glitches.
- ✓ Practice maintaining audience engagement without physical presence.

II. Data-Driven Presentations: Making the Numbers Speak

Data-driven storytelling is becoming increasingly critical. To stand out, focus on:

1. Data Visualization Skills
- ✓ Learn to create compelling charts, graphs, and infographics to make data accessible and memorable.
- ✓ Understand the principles of data storytelling to convey insights effectively.

2. Data Ethics and Privacy
- ✓ Stay informed about data privacy regulations and ethical considerations when using data in presentations.
- ✓ Communicate data sources and methodologies transparently.

3. AI-Assisted Presentation Tools
- ✓ Explore AI-driven tools that can help you analyze data and generate insights for your presentations.
- ✓ Embrace AI-powered speech coaching to improve your delivery.

III. Interactive and Immersive Presentations: Creating Memorable Experiences

The future of presentations is interactive and immersive. Here's how you can prepare:

1. Augmented Reality (AR) and Virtual Reality (VR)
- ✓ Familiarize yourself with AR and VR technologies and their potential for creating immersive presentations.

- ✓ Explore AR/VR presentation tools for storytelling and educational purposes.
2. Gamification
    - ✓ Incorporate gamification elements to engage your audience actively.
    - ✓ Create interactive quizzes, simulations, or virtual tours to enhance learning experiences.
3. Storytelling Through Mixed Media
    - ✓ Combine various media elements, such as videos, animations, and 3D models, to create dynamic presentations.
    - ✓ Use augmented reality to overlay digital content onto the physical world for added impact.

IV. Multicultural and Inclusive Presentations: Navigating Diverse Audiences

In our globalized world, it's crucial to prepare for diverse audiences. Focus on:

1. Cross-Cultural Communication
    - ✓ Develop cultural competence to adapt your message and approach for diverse audiences.
    - ✓ Avoid cultural stereotypes and biases in your presentations.
2. Accessibility
    - ✓ Ensure your presentations are accessible to all, including those with disabilities.
    - ✓ Use accessible design principles for visuals and provide alternative formats when necessary.
3. Language Skills
    - ✓ If presenting in multiple languages, hone your language proficiency to convey nuances accurately.
    - ✓ Use translation and localization services for global presentations.

As the landscape of presentations continues to evolve, embracing change and staying adaptable is key to success. By mastering virtual presentation skills, data-driven storytelling, interactive technologies, and inclusive communication, you can thrive in the digital age and stand out as a confident and influential presenter.

The future of presentations is dynamic and exciting, offering endless opportunities for creativity and innovation. By continually honing your skills and staying attuned to emerging trends, you will be well-prepared to excel in the ever-evolving world of presentations.

Conclusion

As you reach the final pages of this book, you've embarked on a transformative journey through the captivating world of public speaking and presentation skills. We hope that this journey has been insightful, engaging, and above all, empowering.

Throughout the chapters, you've delved deep into the art and science of effective communication. You've learned not only the "hows" but also the "whys" behind every aspect of public speaking. From conquering the fear that often accompanies speaking in public to crafting memorable speeches, and from mastering body language to designing impactful visuals, you've gained a comprehensive understanding of the skill set required to excel in this domain.

The journey you've undertaken is not just about becoming a skilled orator; it's about becoming a confident and influential communicator. It's about recognizing the profound impact that your words, your presence, and your ideas can have on the world around you.

As you reflect on your progress, remember that public speaking is not a static skill. It's a dynamic and ever-evolving journey. The techniques you've learned, the exercises you've practiced, and the wisdom you've gained will serve as your foundation. However, the true mastery of public speaking lies in your willingness to continually refine and expand your skills.

We encourage you to take this journey beyond the pages of this book and into your everyday life. Whether you're a student presenting in class, a professional delivering a critical business proposal, or an advocate championing a cause, your ability to communicate effectively is your superpower.

In your pursuit of confident public speaking, always seek opportunities to practice, refine, and grow. Embrace challenges as stepping stones to growth, and never underestimate the power of continuous improvement. Surround yourself with mentors, peers, and fellow speakers who can offer guidance, feedback, and inspiration.

Remember the lessons of successful speakers who have walked this path before you. Their stories and insights serve as beacons of inspiration, demonstrating that with determination, practice, and unwavering self-belief, you too can make a significant impact with your words.

Ultimately, public speaking is not just a skill; it's a platform for your ideas, your passion, and your voice to resonate with others. It's a conduit for change, influence, and connection in an increasingly interconnected world.

As you move forward in your personal and professional journey, carry with you the knowledge that you have the capacity to inspire, inform, and engage with those around you. Your voice matters, and your ability to use it effectively is a gift that can shape your destiny and the destiny of those who listen.

We wish you boundless success and fulfillment in your pursuit of confident and influential public speaking. May you continue to shine on every stage, inspire every audience, and make a lasting impact on the world.

With warm regards and the utmost belief in your potential,

About the Author
'GERARD ASSEY'

Gerard Assey is a Graduate in Economics, a PGD in Management (HRD) and holds a Doctorate in Leadership. Gerard holds several International Qualifications in Sales, Debt Collection, Training & Teaching, and is a 'Fellow' of the prestigious 'Institute of Sales & Marketing Management'-UK, a Certified NLP Practitioner, a 'Certified Trainer', an 'Accredited Management Teacher-Behavioral Sciences', a 'Certified Competency Facilitator', a 'Certified Management Consultant'- (the International credentials of a professional management consultant, awarded in accordance with global standards of the ICMCI); and a Certification from the University of Michigan in 'Successful Negotiation: Essential Strategies and Skills'

He is also a Member of the 'National Association of Sales Professionals' backed with several years experience in varied industries, both in India and Overseas. He also holds an 'Etiquette Consultant' Certification from the USA (by Sue Fox, Author of Best Seller: 'Business Etiquette for Dummies'. She has trained some of the top celebrities' world over). He was also a recipient of a scholarship for extensive training in Japan on 'Corporate Management for India'.

Gerard Assey is 'Founder & Chief Corporate Trainer' of the Group: **'Citius, Altius, Fortius Unlimited'**- an organization that **celebrated 20 years of Glorious Service** in 2021, focusing on 3 Core Competencies:

People. Performance. Profit; in functional areas of Sales & Marketing, HR & Organizational Development, covering Recruitment, Training & Consultancy!

Having managed organizations with large Sales Forces in India & Overseas, his specialization cover extensive areas of Sales Training (All levels - Presentation, Negotiation, Key/ Strategic Accounts Management & Managerial Skills for all sectors), Bid Proposal/ Capture Planning/ Management Trainings, Retail Sales, Customer Service & Customer Retention Programs, Training for Prevention & Collection of Debt, Self & Personal Development Programs (Time Management, Teamwork & Team Building, Business Etiquette & Personal Grooming, Leadership & Managerial Skills, People Management Skills, Train-the-Trainer etc), including preparation of Custom-designed Business Manuals for Internal (HR, Induction, and Sales etc) & External use (Instruction, User Manuals).

Gerard has successfully conducted over 6000 Trainings & Workshops (as of Oct '23) all across India, Middle East, Africa, Europe & S.E. Asia. Besides public programs conducted regularly, both in India & Overseas, he has some of the top names as clients whom he services from Single Owners to large Public & Government undertakings, covering all sectors, for their in-house needs.

His website: www.CollectionSkills.com is the only one in this part of the world to be featured in the 'Collections & Credit Risk Magazine-USA' under 'Who's Who in Training' and ranks TOP, along with other websites listed below on most search engines.

Gerard is author of 91 books already (Nov 2023),

A few of our business related books:
1. Bite-sized Bits on Commonsense Management
2. Heart to Heart on Life's Principles'
3. How to become a Successful Manager
4. The Sales Professionals' Master Workbook of S.Y.S.T.E.M.S
5. The Professional Business Email Etiquette Handbook & Guide
6. The Professional Business Video-Conferencing Etiquette Handbook & Guide
7. Professional Presentation Skills
8. Exceptional Customer Service
9. Professional Tele-Marketing Skills
10. Professional Debt Collection Skills
11. The G.R.E.A.T. Sales & Service Workbook
12. Sales Training Advantage for Results (*The Ultimate Sales Training Manual to enable you stand out as a S.T.A.R.*)
13. CEO Daily Planner & Organizer
14. The Sales Professionals' Master Daily Planner
15. The Professional Debt Collector's Master Daily Planner
16. My Daily Planner & Organizer
17. MY EMERGENCY INFORMATION RECORD (Family Emergency & Peace of Mind Planner)
18. The Ultimate Therapist & Counselors Planner and Organizer
19. Building an Ethical Workplace
20. Managing Relationships at Work
21. Managing Business Meetings Effectively
22. Effective Delegation Skills
23. Goal Setting for Success
24. B2B Selling by Email
25. Professional Business Etiquette & Grooming
26. Dining Etiquette & Table Manners
27. Effective Networking Skills
28. Grooming, Etiquette & Manners for Teens, Young Adults & Future Leaders
29. Inter-Personal Skills
30. Get Ready, Get Hired!
31. Selling in a Recession
32. Effective Receivables Management in an Economic Downturn!
33. Real Estate & Property Sales Training

Besides regularly contributing to business & trade journals, including international ones such as the 'Creative Training Techniques' and the 'Sales News' of the U.S.A, He is also a member of several prestigious bodies & trade associations, having participated in many Conferences & Workshops in India & Overseas.

Prior to his last assignment of leading & managing a large MNC as head, Gerard had a 3-year stint in the Middle East as a Consultant with a leading British Consultancy Firm.

As the past 'Official Country Representative' for the International Business Award- 'THE STEVIES'-(the business world's own Oscar) for about 4 years- he ensured a few Indian companies that qualify for the same every year!

Gerard can be contacted at:
Email: training@Sales-Training.in,training@CollectionSkills.com
Websites:
        www.Sales-Training.in
        www.EtiquetteWorks.in
        www.CollectionSkills.com
        www.RetailSalesTraining.in
        www.SalesTrainingIndia.com
        www.ManualPreparation.com
        www.TrainingWithPuppets.com
        www.FirstContactAcademy.com
        www.SalesAndMarketingRecruiter.com

Our TRAININGS that can help your team

- ✓ **Sales Effectiveness**: Selling Skills for any Sector: Service/ Logistics/ FMCG Realty/ Insurance & Finance/ Media/ SPA's, Health Clubs & Salons/ Key Account Management, Effective Negotiation Skills/ Bid & Proposal Management Skills/ Retail Sales Training: Any Sector (Auto, Jewelry, Clothing, Luxury etc)
- ✓ **Customer Service Skills**-Complaints Handling & Customer Retention
- ✓ **Debt Prevention & Collection Skills**
- ✓ **Etiquette & Grooming**
- ✓ **Leadership & Managerial Skills**
- ✓ **Self & Personal Development Skills**: Presentation Skills/ Effective Communication Skills/Business Proposal Writing Skills/ Problem Solving & Decision Making Skills/ Empowering Secretaries-The perfect PA! (For Secretaries & PA's)/ Effective Time Management/ Teamwork & Teambuilding/ P.R.I.D.E- **P**ersonal **R**esponsibility **I**n **D**elivering **E**xcellence